Published by:
Ulysses Press
P.O. Box 3440
Berkeley, CA 94703
www.ulyssespress.com

ISBN: 978-1-61243-271-7
Library of Congress Catalog Number 2013957408

Printed in the United States by Bang Printing

10 9 8 7 6 5 4 3 2 1

Acquisitions editor: Keith Riegert
Managing editor: Claire Chun
Editor: Irene Elmer
Proofreader: Lauren Harrison

Distributed by Publishers Group West

Jake & Miller's Big Adventure

A PREPPER'S BOOK FOR KIDS

Written by **Bernie Carr**

Illustrated by **Aja Wells**

 Ulysses Press

The sun was shining into Jake's bedroom. Miller the dog was asleep on the foot of Jake's bed.

Jake got up quietly and pulled on his clothes. He started to search through his closet. He opened drawers. He climbed on a chair to pull things down off of shelves. Bump! Clatter! Thud!

Miller opened one eye. "Jake," he said sleepily, "what are you doing?"

"Get up," said Jake. "Get up and help me get ready."

Miller opened his other eye. He looked alarmed.
"Get ready?" he said. "Get ready for what?"

"Get ready for our adventure," Jake told him. "Today we're going on our big adventure."

Miller looked scared. He said, "I don't like adventures. Let's stay home in bed."

"You'll like this adventure," Jake told him. "It'll be fun."

Miller looked as if he didn't believe it. He said, "Will we be gone a long time? What if we get hungry?"

"Don't worry," Jake told him. "We'll take food. See these backpacks? We'll fill these backpacks full of food."

"Will we take dog biscuits?" said Miller.

"Dog biscuits too," said Jake. "Don't worry. We'll take everything we need."

Jake showed Miller all the food they would take with them. There were dried fruit strips. There was crunchy granola. There was beef jerky. There were dog biscuits and cans of beans.

"All this food will last a long time," Jake said. "That way, we will have enough to eat every day. We may be gone for many days. This is going to be a big adventure."

"Don't forget the can opener," said Miller.

Jake said, "We'll just take a little extra water. When we get thirsty, we'll find places to drink."

"Will it be clean water?" said Miller. "I don't want to drink dirty water."

"Look at this bottle," Jake told him. "This bottle has a filter built in. We'll take this bottle with us so we can drink clean, safe water wherever we go."

"Will it be really, really safe?" said Miller.

"Yes," said Jake. "If the water is dirty, the filter will protect us. The filter makes sure that we won't get sick from the dirty water."

Miller said, "What if there are fish in the water?"

"We'll still be safe," said Jake.

"Where are we going to sleep?" said Miller. "Can I take my bed?"

"We'll sleep in a tent," said Jake. He pulled a tent out of his big pack. "At night we'll set up our tent, and it will be our little home in the woods.

"Sleeping outside is so much fun."

Miller imagined what it would be like to sleep in a tent. He imagined how warm and snug it would be. Outside the tent, it would be dark and cold. Inside the tent, it would be cozy and warm.

"I might like that," he thought.

Snooze & Snug Tent

It was time to decide where they would go on their big adventure.

There was a map of the world in Jake's room. Jake pointed at it.

"We'll go here . . . and here . . . and here," he said. "If we prepare well enough, we could go anywhere."

"We might explore a deep, dark cave," said Jake.

Miller imagined a deep, dark cave. "Will it be really dark, do you think?" he said.

"Don't worry," Jake told him. "We'll have lots of light. We'll take flashlights and headlamps. They'll make everything bright."

"Don't forget the extra batteries," said Miller.

"We might explore a wild jungle," said Jake.

Miller imagined a wild, green, hot jungle. It was full of butterflies and enormous vines.

"What if we get stuck in the vines?" he said. "What if there are snakes?"

"Part of being prepared is being ready for anything. No matter how scary it is," Jake told him.

"If we get stuck in the vines, we'll just climb out. And if there are snakes, we'll walk very, very carefully around them."

"We might get cuts and scratches climbing through all those vines," said Miller.

"We'll be prepared for that too," said Jake. "See this first aid kit? If we get a cut, all we have to do is clean it and put some disinfectant on it and cover it with a bandage."

"There might be bugs," said Miller. "They might bite us."

"See this bug spray?" said Jake.
"That will keep the bugs away."

"Nothing can stop us. Not
even cuts or bugs."

"What will we do when we get tired of walking?" Miller said.

"We'll find a hot-air balloon and fly," said Jake.

Miller imagined going up in a hot-air balloon. Up, up, up. Far, far away. He said, "We might fly so far that we get lost."

"We'll take a compass and a map," Jake told him. "That way we can't get lost."

Miller imagined that they were flying in a hot-air balloon. Up, up, up. Far, far away. He imagined that they were crossing the ocean. He imagined the sun on the water far below.

Miller imagined that the balloon landed in the middle of a great desert. There was nothing but sand, as far as he could see. He imagined that it was very hot.

He imagined that he and Jake began to hike. On and on they hiked through the burning desert.

"Good thing we brought extra water," he told Jake.

Jake said, "We might have to cross cold mountains to get home."

Miller imagined that they were crossing a cold, cold mountain. He imagined that it was covered with snow and ice. He imagined the snow so well that he began to shiver.

Jake said, "Luckily, we're prepared for the cold. I packed us warm sleeping bags and these amazing blankets. They're made of stuff called Mylar, and when you put them over your body, you'll stay warm. You'll stay warm even in the snow and ice."

Miller imagined that they were on the beach. He imagined that they were almost home. He imagined that there was a boat on the shore. They could take the boat to get back home.

But the sky was dark. A storm was coming. Would the storm break before they could get home?

Jake said, "Let's use this crank radio to listen to the weather report. That will tell us how fast the storm is moving."

Miller imagined that they were listening to the weather report. It said that they had just enough time to get home.

The sky was dark. The wind was rising. Miller shut his eyes.

And when he opened his eyes, he was sitting on the floor in Jake's bedroom.

"Well," said Jake. "Are you ready to leave for our big adventure?"

Miller gulped. He thought, "Are we all prepared? Do we have everything we need? Are we ready, no matter what happens?"

"Yes," he thought. "We're ready. This adventure will be fun."

"You bet," he told Jake.

The explorers strapped on their backpacks and they marched out the back door.

And they set up their camp in the backyard.

"We may not be going far," said Miller. "But we're sure ready for anything."

About the Author

Bernie Carr became fascinated with survival techniques and self-sufficiency as a child, hearing stories of her father's adventures in the wilds of Southeast Asia as a land surveyor and avid outdoorsman. As an adult, she developed an interest in emergency preparedness and self-reliance, having survived the 1991 Northridge earthquake in California, the 1992 Los Angeles riots, and the evacuation of her home during the Southern California wildfires. She relocated to Houston, Texas, in an effort to avoid more natural disasters only to arrive in time to encounter the fury of Hurricane Ike in 2008. She is the author of *The Prepper's Pocket Guide* and writes *The Apartment Prepper's Blog* at apartmentprepper.com. Bernie resides in Texas with her family, along with her two cats, Cesar and Cleo.

About the Illustrator

Aja Wells is a professional illustrator who, thanks to Jake and Miller, is now thoroughly prepared to take on anything nature can throw at her. She currently resides in Portland, Oregon. This is her third illustrated book with Ulysses Press.